FUNCTIONING ANXIETY

Unlock the anxiety mystery and take control of your life

by

LUXE LIVING

Table of Contents

We have accepted anxiety and let it into our lives without realizing how much impact it has on our everyday living.

Having trouble sleeping? The answer is an anxious mind. Inconsistent work? Anxiety. People pleasing? The answer is again, anxiety. Over thinkers, insecure people, workaholics. Different categories and yet, the same driving force. Anxiety.

INTRODUCTION

Are anxiety and stress a major problem in your life?

Are you overwhelmed by guilt whenever you prioritize yourself?

If you answered "yes", then that is probably the main reason why you picked up this book. Anxiety and stress can be incredibly difficult to deal with; all of those intense feelings of panic and helplessness, the spiraling thoughts, the quick fix, the momentary relief, then you're back right where you started.

You feel like there is nothing to look forward to, you're not as interested in the things you used to take pleasure in, you struggle to focus or make even the smallest decision. You spend every waking moment inside your head, utterly unable to enjoy the present moment. You live in a constant state of fear, dreading the next anxiety attack.

You're often tense, anxious, and terrified, which pushes you to avoid any situation that might trigger your anxiety. Ironically enough, your avoidance gives you more anxiety because you're afraid of missing out on a life you are incapable of living.

You're exhausted when you go to bed, you're exhausted when you wake up, your mind can't seem to catch a break so you're never able to muster the motivation or energy you need to carry out tasks that are deemed basic and mundane for the majority of people.

Everything is a struggle. It's draining. You want to do better; you want to *be* better. You want to be able to enjoy the little things. You want to push yourself outside your comfort zone, try new things, expand your horizons, open yourself up to the vast world of possibilities at your disposal.

Yet the insidious and debilitating nature of anxiety prohibits you from even entertaining these thoughts in the first place. And so, anxiety becomes a ubiquitous part not only of your life but of your identity as well. You feel condemned to an existence dictated not by your wants and needs but by your fears, worries, and concerns.

The truth is, you may never be able to fully get rid of anxiety. Anyone who claims otherwise would be lying. Nevertheless, you can take back control and live a rewarding and meaningful life outside of the tremors in your mind.

To make this transition, you'll need to learn how to take power away from anxiety so it cannot get in the way of the things you aspire to achieve. This book will help you put an end to that turmoil and suffering.

You can expect to gain a deeper understanding of why you feel, think, and act the way you do when it comes to heightened or stressful situations. You will learn how to overcome guilt, release self-limiting beliefs, and adopt a more kind and forgiving stance towards yourself as well as others around you.

You will also explore the intricacies of anxiety as a survival instinct our ancestors relied on; what was once a tool of self-preservation has become one of self-sabotage. You won't fully get rid of your anxiety, but with the valuable tools in this guide, you will learn to better manage your fears so you can ultimately uncover how to set proper boundaries, make purposeful commitments to yourself, and lead a life that honors your true self; a life in perfect alignment with your core values and principles.

This book is meant to take you on a journey of sorts, a challenging one perhaps, but a rewarding one, nonetheless. The end goal is for you to establish a healthier relationship with yourself, one that doesn't involve loathing, anger, and resentment. Over the course of this book, you will find that the most powerful antidote to these negative feelings is mindful acceptance, kindness, and compassion.

When you detach yourself from all the deeply rooted fears, worries, and anxieties, you're also freeing up space for you to discover your true values and the things that matter to you the most. Because, at the end of the day, it's these things that will guide you forward into the life you want to live.

As that space continues to expand, you will learn how to redirect your energy and focus on the people and experiences that allow you to grow, spread your wings, and free yourself from the shackles and constraints of your past.

So, are you ready to take back control of your life?

CHAPTER 1

What does it really mean to be anxious?

Anxious brains:

Fear, love, worry, and anxiety are all feelings we have as humans. In fact, if it weren't for these feelings, we would not have prepared ourselves better for tomorrow or made strides to be technologically and socially efficient. If you've ever wondered what it's like to be anxious, then you've probably already felt it. Fear and worry about the future are something that everyone, regardless of their background, will experience at some point in their life. In fact, fear and anxiety are actually useful. Yes, I know! Anxiety and worry have probably saved your life at some point without you even realizing it. Fear is not just a mental state - it actually prepares you quite well for the future. Feeling anxiety gets your body ready for challenges that may put your body at risk. But here is the catch. This risk was prevalent thousands of years ago when we had to ward off predators, protect our land, chase away enemies at our village borders, and brace for food shortages in the winter. Now unless you're a time traveler, you probably never have to worry about these things in your life.

Our brain is extremely intelligent, and while you may think it's sometimes stupid because it makes you anxious when you're literally in your comfy room with no threat of danger, that's because we no longer need those "alerts".

Our brain is pretty ancient, and it worked amazingly well back when we were hunter-gatherers. For instance, we have an impressive response to danger which was very common back in the day. We are also subject to Dunbar's number; the notion that our brain has a cognitive limit when it comes to stable relationships which is supposedly around 150 (Dunbar, 1992). You've probably met a lot more than this number, but we did not meet this number of people when we were hunter-gatherers. The number was probably 70 to 90 people that you met in your whole life and it was usually the same people you met from the day of your birth until the day you died. The way our brain worked was impressive and it made us into who we are today. We lived this way for anywhere between 150,000 years to 320,000 years. One simple discovery rapidly changed the way we lived which was relatively very recent: around 8,000 years ago. Agriculture was discovered, and this meant that we no longer had to rely on hunting, which was not only time consuming, but also quite costly as it risked a lot of lives. We could farm animals like goats and cows, we had crops, and plenty of time on our hands. A lot of scientists and archeologists believe that this was the precursor to our civilization as we had the chance to use our big brain capabilities.

So, what was the outcome? A very advanced civilization compared to when we were hunter-gatherers, with a brain that is ancient and has not evolved for the way we live today. Sure, anxiety is important when real danger is imminent, but do we really need to be anxious about replying to a text on the phone or when ordering food at a restaurant?

Anxiety is the most common mental health problem in the US as more than 65 million Americans will experience anxiety at some point in their life. (Hirschtritt, et al 2015).

Fear is important and it can literally save your life on many occasions, but when fear is misplaced or excessive, it is no longer useful. In fact, anxiety is mostly harmful. Instead of being proactive, anxiety takes hold of you and makes you think about the worst possible outcome.

When anxiety is actually good:

Stress is labeled as a bad thing, and it should be for the most part. But a little bit of anxiety is actually good for you. The constant worry and anticipation of future events can make us motivated and excited about life. Anxiety gives you an incentive to go out and do things. Anxious about your job interview? Research the company history or rehearse answers to the most common interview questions. Worried about the exam? Read more and work harder.

Even when anxiety is about danger, it can serve as an indication that something is wrong. While you might feel anxious about your relationship all of a sudden, this may mean something when it comes to your significant other. Your anxiety might be sudden or violent, but it isn't always irrational or misplaced. Your anxiety might be amplified and intense, but it might be because something is going on that your subconscious has picked up on.

How anxiety feels:

As we have established, anxiety is quite normal, but what is not normal is excessive and misplaced anxiety. Anxiety is best described as crippling because that's what it is. Let's be honest, good anxiety is one that makes you work hard to finish whatever work you have, it makes you avoid dangerous situations and helps you act.

Let's go over what anxiety feels like. Anxiety makes you so

overwhelmed with the unknown that you do not want to do anything at all. You become so obsessed with knowing the future and how bad things could get that you do not want anything to happen in the future. It's an internal tug-of-war that you are having for no reason at all. Because anxiety is so powerful, you often feel anxious about anxiety itself. Since anxiety has caused you so much harm in your life, you start to worry that it will cause more harm and before you know it, it's there again.

Anxiety is not always mental; it can be physical as well. Oddly enough, as anxious as you are about the future, you're so fatigued. You become very irritable about everything, and nausea starts to overwhelm you. This can often be associated with some abdominal cramping and pain. Your body in this state is ready for battle; you imagine scenarios in your head that might happen in the future, and this becomes your reality. The overwhelming fear of what's to come is holding you hostage for the future that is always looming over your head.

Anxiety really becomes a monster when it overwhelms you and starts to take shape. It all starts with feeling anxiety in your head, but it often destroys your relationships - not because of your own actions, but because of the fear of what your actions may cause in the future. Your brain tells you there is a form of danger out there to get you, but it won't tell you what it is, why it's dangerous, when it's going to come, or how it's going to come about. This may seem illogical, but using logic with anxiety is completely counterproductive. Logic does not work with anxiety because it is in your own head. You cannot rationalize something when your own brain is making you think that this is all real.

Your brain starts to create problems that don't exist and never will. Your brain is anticipating a threat coming soon. It's almost like knowing that a villain in a story is going to appear and cause chaos because their on-set track is playing in the background. The only problem is that the villain never comes but the OST is still playing.

The result of this feeling is that anxiety is not only going to make you worried about the future and about anxiety itself, but it is also going to make you feel exhausted. Anxiety makes your brain be in alert mode at all times for no reason and if you've ever been anxious for a small period of time, then you know how mentally exhausting it can be.

Signs you have anxiety:

Excessive worry:

We all worry about many things in our lives, but too much worry isn't always a good thing. When you worry too much and too often, this is a sign that you have anxiety. This is especially true when the worry is sudden or triggered by everyday normal and casual events.

Being restless:

Anxiety can be manifested physically when your body is in a state of fight or flight. It can often be described as an uncomfortable urge to suddenly move. This is often a symptom that happens after being 'mentally' anxious. If you experience restlessness and you feel like you want to suddenly move around, then you probably have anxiety.

Irritability:

It's common for people who have generalized anxiety disorders to experience irritability when they are in anxiety episodes. They might suddenly not want to deal with anything or anyone all for no real reason.

Tight muscles:

Unlike having tight muscles after a hard workout, anxiety causes your muscles to feel tense and twitchy. This is believed to be due to the fact that anxiety causes the brain to signal to the body that it's time to take action, which causes your muscles to twitch and work.

Panic attacks:

Panic attacks cause the person who is experiencing them to have an intense episode of overwhelming fear and worry. This is often debilitating and can cause your body to feel numb. You might feel like you cannot breathe and that your chest is shrinking into itself. The overwhelming fear that you cannot breathe causes your panic attacks to be more intense because they are now fueled by a real threat which is the risk of not being able to breathe.

Irrational fears:

It's completely normal to be afraid of lions, spiders, snakes, or fire hazards. However, irrational fears are just irrational, and they do not make any sense. Phobias of being in an open space, using transportation, being in your home alone, or being outside, in general, are a clear indication that you have an irrational fear. When fear is justified, such as being afraid of fire hazards, then it's fine. But when it does not make sense that you fear being in your own home, then that's a sign you have anxiety.

Twitching:

While twitching can be caused by having tight muscles, it's

usually due to anxiety. If you're resting with no threat whatsoever yet still feel like your face is twitching or your muscles are ready to spring to action, then there is a high chance you have anxiety.

The bottom line:

Anxiety is an essential emotion that we are all familiar with. However, too much of it can certainly take its toll on our mental health and performance. There are obvious benefits to being anxious about the future, but there is always a limit. There are a lot of symptoms and dead giveaways when it comes to anxiety which everyone should be aware of. Anxiety can definitely make you feel like you're trapped inside your own mind, unable to break free. So how come? Why would we fear irrational everyday moments and be anxious to death about something as simple as going for a walk at sunset? Well, the answer to that question may be rooted in our own ancient brain that we talked about earlier. The next chapter will discuss this idea further and look at exactly why and how we are so anxious.

CHAPTER 2

Anxious ancestors, anxious us

At first glance, it seems that anxiety is a trait that humans should have been able to get rid of through evolution. Natural selection weeds out those that cannot survive and gives power to those that adapt. So why is anxiety still wired in our brains? Could it have been a missing link, or is it actually one of the reasons why we evolved to be the apex on earth?

It turns out that anxiety is there for a good reason. Anxiety is a danger alarm to cause your body to react to threats. It can be anticipated, and we humans have been able to develop very good anticipation skills for threats. Our ancestors relied on the skills that anticipate danger and threats in order to be better prepared for the future. For our ancestors, anxiety was normal, and they just felt it as a reaction to danger just as we feel full after a good hearty meal. However, most of the anxiety we feel today is still a threat alarm, except that this threat is like a smoke detector going off after you slightly burn the toast for breakfast.

The curse of our brain:

Our brain is likely the number one reason why we are alive today and thriving. A lot of evolutionary biologists believe that switching from walking on all feet to being bipedal (walking) has allowed us more time to use our hands for tools. These tools helped us develop weapons to protect our tribes from predators and hunt animals. It also helped us create fire which was revolutionary. Due to the fact that we could cook our food and process it with fire, our digestive system no longer needed as much energy to metabolize foods, and all the energy that was left went straight to our brain. Our brains became much more developed as we began to use more tools and developed more complex social communities. Little by little, the sentient human brain became a lot more complex with improved memory and cognition.

With our brain gaining a lot more power, we gained an ability that transformed the future of our race and that is the ability to imagine. Think about it; imagination is the most defining feature that sets us apart from all other creatures. The ability to think and ponder about the future allowed us to visualize events that might occur in the future. As a group of ancient ancestors, we had the ability to think about our next raid against a herd of buffalo or ways to store meat for the winter. This ability to think about the future and prepare for what is to come is crucial when it comes to our survival as a species. As the brain realizes that danger might come at any time, a neurochemical reaction chain starts to occur in the brain, pumping your sympathetic nervous system into overdrive mode. Your brain commands more blood flow to your muscles, your vision narrows and sharpens, and your muscles start to twitch from the amount of energy that they have stored. This would be very useful if you had to run away from a predator or if you had to take down the woolly mammoth, but not useful when you are in a crowded elevator or when you are discussing a pay rise with your boss.

Thinking about future events was very useful, and we needed it as a feature of our complex brain. However, this brain that we are talking about is optimized for the hunter-gatherer and ancient ancestors. Humans are not only the only species that can think about the future, but they are the only ones that can trigger a fight or flight response when there is no apparent immediate danger.

Anxiety is one of those byproducts of being alert and aware about the future and it is essential. With the feeling of anxiety about not having enough food for winter, we can hunt more animals in the summer and find ways to store food. If we enter new territory, we get anxious and elevate our senses so we are better prepared for a sudden attack from predators. This all fine, but as humans who live in the 21st century, your biggest worry in the day is probably going to be avoiding traffic on your way to work.

Humans today with ancient brains:

The term ancient brain might give you the idea that our brain is useless and old, but in reality, our brains are actually a lot more complex than you think and we are still tapping into their potential. The discovery of fire was an enormous step in the right direction which helped us develop our brains. However, agriculture has got to be the single most important discovery we have made.

Crops and plants did not need that much energy to be harvested, unlike hunting animals which took away so many resources. With agriculture, humans were able to think about a lot of other things such as how to protect themselves, how to make food, and how to grow as a tribe. Farming was also very useful, as humans no longer needed to find animals and hunt them down.

A few centuries later, humans began thinking about deeper concepts, created the concept of gods, deities, morality, and religion.

Fast forward even more and you have us in the 21st century. The only curse is that we still have some of the built-in features that are no longer needed. Anxiety is proof that we were highly efficient when it came to thinking about the future. However, the disorder of anxiety is a different story. We do not need to be anxious all the time about a threat that will never come.

The difference between us and a water buffalo, for example, is that the buffalo does not have to think about the future. They are constantly grazing the land and eating whatever comes their way. It is not until a lion pounces on them that they have the fight or flight response. Our brain can do the fight or flight response without having a lion pounce on us which is why anxiety is so prevalent.

Anxiety amplified today:

The issue with anxiety is that we live in a delayed return environment that is full of doubt and anticipation. For instance, a cat that lives in an instant return environment will come to you to get food because you provide it. When the cat feels tired, it will just sleep. However, we live in an element of uncertainty that is always looming over us. For instance, we might work in a company, but we are always worried about being laid off or whether we might mess something up.

We have so many variables at play at the same time that we think about constantly. The way we handle life is that we imagine those scenarios in our head and adapt accordingly. The only issue is that this is even worse for our anxious brains. Because our brain is so sensitive to stimuli that danger, the smallest hint of threat, can trigger a fight or flight response and get us all riled up as if a bear is chasing us in the wild.

Our brain is not designed to cope with all these little variables, and we just cannot turn it off. It would be great if we could control how we feel and what we are worried about, but our brains just won't work like that. They are constantly worrying about immediate dangers that might pop up at any time.

Is anxiety useful in our biology?

One of the most interesting things that happens when we are stressed needs to be brought up. Anxiety is not just in your head; it's actually in your body as well. Have you ever noticed that threats are not always in your head? Stress can often make you feel tired, groggy, sleepless, and agitated. This is all normal, as the brain signals to the body that something bad is going to happen because there is danger. For instance, when we encounter danger, there is a high likelihood that we will get wounded which is not the best thing to happen to you in the wild. Pathogens and germs can wreck your body from the inside and cause severe illness or even death.

Our brain basically depends on our perception of threats to activate certain functions in the body. For instance, if your brain signals anxiety, it will know that something might happen and trigger an inflammatory response in case you get wounded. This is what (Raison &Miller, 2012) noticed in a piece of research that looked at the evolutionary significance of depression in pathogens. In other words, the mere perception of stress will activate functions in the immune system that are supposed to defend the body from pathogens. Overall, this mechanism is very useful, and has probably saved hundreds of thousands of our ancestors. However, it's really not that useful to us in today's modern world.

The bottom line:

Anxiety is an essential feeling and reaction that we have developed for a long time thanks to evolution. Our perception of danger can prepare us for the future, and this is likely something that was useful in everyday hunter-gatherer ancestors. The only issue is that we still have the function of anxiety today which can interfere with our everyday life. This is especially true in today's world that is full of possibilities and the unknown, which amplifies our anxiety even more. Anxiety has lingered on as a part of us and it has some serious side effects that will be discussed in the following chapter. The buildup of thoughts, the burning fear about the future, and the worry about what we can or cannot do creates a new state of danger reaction that is neither fight nor flight and that is freeze. Anxiety is known for causing a serious buildup of thoughts and feelings that are all toxic and negative. Find out more about this in the next chapter.

CHAPTER 3

Buildup of thoughts and feelings

If you have ever experienced anxiety, then you're probably familiar with the build-up of thoughts and feelings. We all worry about things that are coming up in our lives. We might have exams, job interviews, we might be working on a project or striving to do something that is hard. Anxiety is normal in those cases as it prepares your mind for what is to come and helps you imagine scenarios but this is where the vicious cycle starts when it comes to anxiety. This buildup of anxiety that involves our feelings can be very intense and cause severe trauma which can haunt your mental health. Not to mention, it's completely counterproductive. While anxiety should prepare you for the worst and make your imagination more flexible for future events, the overwhelming fear we have about the future can paralyze us and send us deeper into a very dark place.

The dark cycle of emotions and thoughts:

There are a lot of ways that anxiety can be built up and started. One of the most common ways is when anxiety starts out of nowhere due to a minor event in your life. It usually starts with a few conflicts until something bothers you and you start to worry about it for the next few days. For instance, you might develop anxiety that is triggered by elevators. So, every time you are in an elevator, you will feel that your anxiety is sky-high. Anxiety can get you even if you do not go to an elevator; the thought of having to use an elevator because you're going out can cause your thoughts to spiral out of control. You start to worry about nothing and create scenarios in your head that are fictional. In your head, these scenarios are real, and they will happen. So, if you create a scenario of you having to go into a crowded elevator with eight people and go ten floors up, your brain starts to quite literally create the same atmosphere for the elevator anxiety. You start to blush, sweat, get irritated, develop tight chest syndrome, and breathe very slowly. You're still in your room and haven't gone out yet, but all of a sudden the anxiety has paralyzed you from moving to the point that you cannot go out anymore. But wait, there is more. You start to get anxious about not going out as well; how bad it would be to not have food for the next couple of days because you didn't go to the grocery store, what if a hurricane hit my town, what if we have an earthquake and I have no food to eat before rescue comes? All of a sudden, we went from a small worry about a tiny inconvenience into a scenario that our brain thinks is real and is happening.

The dark cycle of emotions and thoughts can start out of nowhere and with no triggers whatsoever. You might not even think about a trigger, but you will still feel the anxiety build up. In fact, you might be totally normal at one point but you start to get anxious about getting anxious. You might be about to have a job interview for a career you have always wanted, but your brain says: "You know what would be really bad? Getting all anxious and panicky in the interview". You start to think about how bad it would be to get anxious and how it would totally destroy your chances and make you look nervous. The scenarios in your head start to emerge again and then you start to truly get anxious about getting anxious and here it is again.

What the buildup looks like:

Anxiety thinking build up can start in a lot of ways, especially if you're prone to getting anxiety. There are several types of irrational thoughts to look out for which can be detrimental to your mental health. Here are a few of them:

Catastrophes: Anxious people have a tendency to think about the absolute worst possible scenario that could ever happen. It's similar to the way that the writers for the Final Destination series create their scenes. Enjoying a nice road trip in the summer? Maybe not - a truck full of sharply-cut logs pulls up in front of you and you know the rest. This can really ruin your life and make every experience miserable because you're always worried about when the catastrophe is going to happen. A small headache from drinking less coffee can make you think that you have a brain tumor. If your heart skips a beat, you start to think it's a heart attack.

Negativity: Another common trope that anxious people fall into is negative filtering. For instance, you might go on a date, but you have a small pimple that is hidden. Your brain won't think that it's hidden, it will make you think that your date is looking at that pimple and thinking about how bad it looks.

Black and white thinking: Every anxious person is guilty of this at some point. The binary thinking that there is either black or white, 1 or 0, bad or good, perfect or terrible, pure or contaminated can make your life miserable. For instance, you might have received a comment about taking small speech breaks when giving a presentation and this makes you think that your presentation was terrible and awful. But you did not look at the fifteen other positive reviews telling you how insightful your presentation was.

Depression and anxiety: Prepare for trouble and make it double

You think that anxiety is bad enough? Wait 'til you hear how it's usually compounded with other mental issues. Anxiety is generally a 'high-energy' state while depression is a 'low-energy' state. You'd think that those two never meet, but there is huge correlation. Most people who suffer from depression also suffer from anxiety and the reverse is also true.

Most anxious people know how dreadful it is to be anxious which causes to them to be aware of their miserable predicament. This inevitably causes the person to feel depression about having anxiety and how much the latter has ruined life for them. Additionally, depression itself causes anxiety and amplifies it.

In fact, anxiety and depression can be treated by the same medications which use anti-depressants to mitigate the effects of both conditions. Around two thirds of people who have anxiety also have major depression. About two thirds of people who have depression also report a lot more anxiety. When looking at the symptoms of anxiety such as restlessness, irritability, lack of sleep, lack of focus, they are also found in people who have depression.

So, the question is, why are these always together? A lot of researchers have come up with different ideas but one of the most prevalent ideas related to stress triggers. The fight or flight response is one of the most powerful primal instincts in the body and it's both mental and physical. When you really think about this, anxiety and depression are just a different type of "flight". Anxiety is a state of restlessness and depression is a state of hopelessness. In the biochemical sense, the fight or flight response involves a supernova of hormones that prepare the body for danger or trauma. It turns out that people who have a specifically-heightened sense of stress triggers can feel those emotions on a much stronger scale. In other words, anxiety and depression are two sides of the same coin when it comes to responding to stress.

When it comes to anxiety, the stress response is that of stillness when a threat is perceived. It's a form of flight or freeze. Depression is a response that also involves stillness but in a hopeless sense as opposed to anxiety which involves helplessness. It can be hard to link both of them as they seem so different, but again, they are just different sides of the same coin.

Negative talk in anxiety can further show how it blinds the person to the 'good options' and only shows the possibilities that are catastrophic. Overall, the spiral of thoughts and feelings is quite vicious and calls for treatment.

The bottom line:

Anxiety involves a serious buildup of thoughts and feelings. It's a nasty cycle that can make you feel hopeless and really put you in a dark place. It can also involve other mental issues such as depression which is another common illness that can be linked to anxiety.

CHAPTER 4

Why me?

You've probably asked yourself this question in a bad anxiety episode; "why me?". The reason why this question is so hard to answer is really that there isn't a clear solution. Anxiety can feel like a curse, especially when it causes you hardships in your life and the only thing you can ask yourself is "why me?". So, let's dive deeper into that because it can actually answer a lot of questions about anxiety and mental disorders in the brain.

Why you have anxiety:

You've probably asked yourself one, if not all of these questions: "Why do I have these anxiety problems?"

"Why can't I control my anxiety?"

"Why did I develop my anxiety?"

"Why am I not like other people who have normal anxiety levels?"

"Did I do something that caused my anxiety?"

"Did I inherit anxiety?"

Genetics vs. experiences:

Most people suspect that their anxiety might be inherited. If anxiety disorders are linked to brain chemistry, then that means there is a component that drives the brain chemistry disorder genetically. The answer to the question of whether anxiety is genetic or based on experience is both. Most anxiety disorders have a genetic component to them, but they can be influenced by outside factors such as daily stresses. In other words, your anxiety can be "awakened".

Your brain inherits a lot of components from your parents which includes the brain chemistry that controls how you feel. So, what does this all mean? Well, the main point is that anxiety can be genetic, but it's triggered by events in your everyday life. This means that that some people are more prone to getting anxiety than others. So, while you get so much anxiety for a minor event, there are people who can handle so much anxiety with no problem.

Am I cursed because of my genetics and biology?

A person's genetics influence much of their brain structure and function. Although the scientific community and academia do not have a full understanding of anxiety in the brain, there is a general consensus that anxiety can be genetic. Catherine Pittman, Ph.D., a clinical psychologist who works with the ADAA, argues that the majority of a person's anxiety is genetic. There are also structural and functional differences in the brain of a person who has anxiety when compared to a normal brain. Though these differences are not as dramatic, they do contribute and validate the involvement of genetics in the issue of anxiety.

Therefore, you should probably look at your close family. Do you see your parents or close relatives having frequent panic attacks? Anxiety symptoms or other mental health issues? If so, the anxiety you have could be genetic, and the answer to the question "why me?" could be because of your family.

The true reason for this brain chemistry disorder is due to the small size of amygdalas when compared to normal brains (Milham et al, 2005). In addition to that, it was seen that individuals who have frequent anxiety episodes and panic attacks are more likely to have a missing serotonin receptor which a lot of researchers believe may be the cause of anxiety (Neumeister et al, 2004).

Can a person's experiences cause anxiety disorders?

While genetics may play a role in how your brain is structured and how it functions, a person's experiences may have an even bigger impact on the level of anxiety they have. While some people are more prone to getting anxiety than others due to their biology, we have to remember that we all have anxiety to some extent. Anxiety exists in every single one of us and it can be triggered for everyone. People who live a very high-stress life are more prone to becoming more anxious.

It's not only the lifestyle of the person, but also their past experiences that can contribute to the level of anxiety they have. For instance, traumatic experiences are quite powerful when it comes to the level of anxiety someone will experience in the future. In fact, studies have shown that the brain will create trauma out of nowhere if it has experienced trauma before. (Bremmer et al, 2003).

The trauma that someone experiences in life can have a very big impact on the way the brain functions. Because these traumatic experiences are so powerful, they can create a lasting effect on a person's mental health. For instance, a person who had a car accident will constantly have anxiety about being in a car. Therefore, it's clear that your experiences can cause the brain to be anxious.

Negative experiences such as car accidents, sexual assault, dog attacks, or events that cause our brain to react violently can literally have the same effect as our own biology.

In a very interesting study that was done to further explore this topic, it was seen that experiences and biology can be interchangeable. For instance, biology itself can control experiences, but experiences can also control biology (Kilpatrick et al, 2007). PTSD was seen to be genetic after a traumatic hurricane. Individuals who did not have anxiety before started having anxiety after the hurricane and passed it down to their children. The gene expression after the hurricane raised a lot of questions about the understanding of anxiety and the brain.

Drawing from these scientific findings, a lot of people believe that despite having the genes that make someone more anxious, it is possible that they can live without anxiety if their experiences and environment permit it. Not only that, but it is also possible that they won't pass down the genes that cause someone to be more anxious. Other conclusions can be made from these findings (Kilpatrick et al, 2007), that gene expression is not always active unless they do not have the support. In the example of the traumatic hurricane experience, people who had the gene for PTSD did not always have PTSD unless they had a traumatic experience where they did not have social support.

Experiences such as rape, sexual abuse, child abuse, trauma, and physical violence are more likely to make a person more anxious even if they have do not have the gene expression that makes them more anxious. In other words, your experiences are just as influential as your genes when it comes to how much anxiety you will have. Therefore, you are not doomed to have an anxious life if you have the genes that make you more anxious. This is good news because your experiences and what you do in life can be changed while you cannot change what genes you have in the brain.

Back to the question:

If we go back and ask the question of "why me?", it's highly likely that it's one of two scenarios; the first being that you have inherited this from your family. The second is that you have had experiences that changed the way you think and function altogether. So, if you had a hard experience that was very traumatic, it might still be affecting the way you think today and is something that you should consider.

However, it is very likely that anxiety starts to become a problem after a specific event or issue. So, you have to look back in your life and think about the time when you started to develop anxiety. It would help immensely if you had been journaling and writing about your life and how you felt. The reason for that is because even people who have the genes for anxiety do not get anxiety until a specific event in their life. This event does not have to be singular or short; it can be a phase or multiple events at once where you experienced trauma that may have triggered your anxiety.

Are there ways to control how I am?

Unless you have a time machine where you can prevent your past self from experiencing trauma or if you have a superpower that controls specific genes, then you probably will not be able to change the way you are. In fact, you should not. Everyone has different experiences that are unique to them, and will shape their understanding of the world differently. There are no such things as perfect genes or a perfect life.

So, the question really becomes "are there ways that I can control my predicament?". The answer is yes. First, the brain can change over time, and it can adapt. Although not all brains are equal, we have seen cases where the brain is able to teach itself to be less anxious through learning to control its understanding of 'threat'. Since anxiety is basically a response to a threat, we can control how much we get it once we encounter those threats. Regardless of how serious or mundane these threats are, we can change how we perceive them and how we react to them. Moreover, we can also change how our brain goes about hormone secretion once a threat has been identified in the brain. This can be done through medication that improves the secretion of hormones such as serotonin and can have a lot of benefits in the way we perceive the world as well as our happiness levels.

The bottom line:

It's common to ask yourself the question of "why me?". In simple words, the reason why you have anxiety is probably twofold. The first is because you have it in your brain through genetics, and the second is from previous experiences. However, having anxiety in the brain does not make you doomed to have it. In fact, there are a lot of ways we can control anxiety and how we perceive it which will be discussed in the next chapter.

CHAPTER 5

Solutions and rules

Usually right around the time you feel depressed and mad over the fact that you are the way you are as an anxious person, you start to look at things from a different perspective. Instead of resenting your experiences and genes, you start to look at the solutions. Being proactive is very important when it comes to anxiety and having an open mind is crucial. This chapter will discuss the steps that you can take to treat anxiety as well as some rules to follow in order to ensure that you are on the right path.

The two main ways to treat anxiety:

There are two main causes of anxiety: genes and experiences. What this means is that your chemistry and your thoughts are what control your anxiety. If you are an anxious person, it's probably because you suffer from a chemical imbalance in the brain. Happiness can be expressed outside, but all happiness is just a chemical reaction in your brain that drive 'good feel' hormones such as dopamine and serotonin to the brain which make you feel happy. Being anxious is pretty much the same thing; it's a chemical process.

The two main ways to treat anxiety have to do with your brain chemistry. The way we can have access to the brain chemistry is through actively altering it using medications that seek to increase the level of certain hormones like serotonin or dopamine. However, this isn't the only way to change the chemistry since we know brain chemistry can be accessed through physical activity. What this means is that experiences are equally as important.

Chemical intervention:

The first thing we are going to discuss is how anxiety can be treated with the chemistry of the brain. There are different types of medication that you can choose from, which will have more or less the same effect on your anxiety level. If your doctor decides that you should take one of them, then there is a good chance that it's worth it. Regardless of what type of medication you choose, there should be monitoring on a constant basis in order to ensure that you're making consistent progress. So, let's go over the main types of anxiety medications.

<u>Anti-depressants:</u>

Although these medications are mostly made for depression, they can be used to improve mood and stress levels. In addition to that, there is a good chance that you will want to have an anti-depressant anyway because most people who have anxiety also suffer from some form of depression.

(SSRIs) are selective serotonin reuptake inhibitors as well as serotonin-norepinephrine reuptake inhibitors. The way they work is by increasing the brain's level of serotonin which is a type of transmitter that cells use to communicate. A good level of serotonin ensures that the brain communicates more efficiently, which has been proven to be effective when it comes to treating anxiety and its symptoms. In fact, there is a good amount of evidence that shows y that a brain that communicates efficiently is less likely to be depressed (Martin et al, 2009).

Anti-depressants can also be used for all types of anxiety disorders since they improve how the brain works. However, they're not the be all and end all of anxiety medication since some people may experience side effects.

Benzodiazepines:

If you've ever done research on anxiety medication, then you've probably stumbled upon this term before. It's a very well-known type of medication for many types of anxiety. The difference between benzodiazepines and anti-depressants is how fast they work. While anti-depressants may take some time to kick in, benzodiazepines work fast. However, you may also develop a tolerance to benzodiazepines.

The main way they work is by targeting (GABA) gamma-aminobutyric acid. This in effect can calm down a fast-paced brain. In addition to treating anxiety, benzodiazepines also treat panic disorders, social anxiety, and mood disorders. However, benzodiazepines may have some side effects, such as drowsiness, muscle weakness, and dizziness. If side effects persist, then you should discuss with your psychiatrist other options such as the next one.

Beta-blockers:

These medications take a completely different approach when it comes to anxiety treatments. As the name implies, they block certain chemical signals from entering the nervous system and operating as beta receptors. They can help you even prevent anxiety itself which can be a great tool to use if you are in a pinch.

Non-medicinal ways to treat anxiety:

Medicine may be important and even crucial for anxiety. However, it isn't the only option. In fact, it is better to treat anxiety using both medication and lifestyle changes.

Moving forward:

One of the ways that anxiety can make you stagnate in life is when it handicaps your movement. If you let anxiety stop you from moving out both literally and figuratively, then you're letting it win. Movement is not only important for blood circulation which can help the brain function better, but it is also important for mentally feeling like you're getting somewhere.

The best way to do this is to get into exercise. This is a great way to beat anxiety and even counter some of the side effects that are known in most medications. Physical activity is great for improving endorphins and serotonin levels in the brain which are very important for how you feel. It helps you get out of your head for a while and make you focus on performance. For instance, you can't really have spiraling thoughts and anxiety over running because the best way to go about running is to go forward. You might not notice this consciously, but your brain will subconsciously realize this and act accordingly. In addition to that, exercise can help you progress in some type of endeavor.

Improve your sleep:

Most people will think about sleeping more when sleeping better, but that's not the full story. Sleeping 7-9 hours is crucial, but a quality 7-hour sleep session is a million times better than a 10-hour sweaty, bumpy sleep in a noisy room with a lot of light. It's just as important to look after your sleep quality and work on things such as getting sleep in a chilled, pitch-black room with very little distraction. Sleep is one of the times when the body works on itself to recover and heal.

Don't caffeine your way out of life:

One of the habits that a lot of us are guilty of is consuming a lot of caffeine because we're so stressed and haven't slept well. But that is like putting a Band-Aid on a gaping wound. While coffee once in a while can be great, you should not use it to mask the lack of sleep. Not to mention, caffeine can destroy your sleep quality and make you so much more anxious.

Chase away negativity:

Do you want to know the best way to get rid of anxiety? Get rid of what makes you anxious in the first place. This isn't about having a 'safe space' or shielding yourself from the real world. It's about protecting your mental state. It's fine to go out there and be stressed at work because it's necessary, but if your whole life is stressed and you deal with negativity all the time, then it's probably time for a change. Look for sources that cause negativity in your life and chase them away. You cannot afford to be anxious all the time for absolutely no reason. Unfortunately, this may mean that you have to cut off or limit how much time you spend with some close people.

Establish your boundaries:

Anxious people have a bad habit of not saying no and it destroys their mental state. Boundaries are very important for your wellbeing, since they allow you to establish where you begin and where the other ends. Being able to say no is also great for your mental state. This isn't about being mean or anything; it's about you and how you feel. Remember, your plate is only so big, and you cannot make everyone happy.

Work on your nutrition:

One of the best ways to improve your brain chemistry without using medication is by making sure you are eating well. A lot of people really don't know the power of nutrition and how much it can help. Make sure you are eating a diet that contains a good amount of protein, healthy fats, and moderate carbohydrates. You should also eat a lot of vegetables and fruits to ensure that you get enough nutrients. You can also take vitamin D3, zinc, magnesium, iron, vitamin C, vitamin B6, B12, and a multivitamin.

How to change your thoughts from anxious thinking to normalized thinking:

In order for you to get over anxiety, a mental shift is necessary. The reason for this is because without changing how you think about yourself and your experiences in life, it would be very hard to make any changes. The challenge then becomes not about changing, but about tricking your mind. Luckily, there are a few ways you can go about this in order to get rid of anxious thinking.

The first thing that needs to be said is that changing your mindset is not a one-time-only event. Forget about the Hollywood light bulb moment when the protagonist suddenly finalizes their role and becomes the best version of themselves like a light switch. Instead of looking at it as a light switch, you should look at it as a sunrise. First, there is the overwhelming darkness of dusk. Then you start to see the darkness fade away slowly but surely with the dawn until you see the sunrise. After this, you see the sun in all its glory in the middle of the day. It's a slow transition; just like how it is with changing your mindset around anxiety. You don't just get a light bulb moment and do a 180. It takes time, effort, and consistency.

Now, let's talk about ways to change that mindset. First, we have to address our anxious thoughts. The first important thing is to identify anxious thoughts. Anxiety tends to overestimate the length, frequency, and intensity of the bad events happening in our lives. In fact, anxiety is so good at making us dwell on these variables that the likelihood of the bad event happening starts to become unquestionable. Anxiety makes us overestimate how bad things are going to be which can put us under a lot of initial stress. So, the best thing to do is to just ask yourself these questions.

What would happen if my anxiety actually became a reality?

How do I know for sure that this is even a possibility?

What is the most likely outcome of this situation?

What is the absolute worst that can happen?

These questions may seem like they can trigger even more anxiety, but in reality, they challenge the act of anxious thinking. More likely than not, you are going to have to remind yourself that this is the anxiety we're talking about and not real life. By identifying that you are having anxiety and that it is actually altering the way you think, you will start to overcome this issue and come out on top.

10 rules for anxiety management:

Rule 1: Re-label what is happening

One of the ways to fool anxiety is by recounting what is happening. This works like magic sometimes. By literally just saying what is happening and almost telling it like a story, it starts to make a lot more sense and becomes less mysterious and anxiety-inducing. Instead, by verbalizing your situation, it becomes more real and vivid.

Rule 2: Big deep breaths

You might not realize it while it's happening, but it's very important that you breathe in and out deeply. By making sure you get enough oxygen to the brain, you can process your thoughts a lot better.

Rule 3: Follow the 3-3-3 technique

Whenever you feel like anxiety is getting the best of you and you might have a panic attack soon, use this technique. First, name three things you see, this could be your phone, a magazine, or a cup of tea. Then name three sounds you hear in the background. Finally, move three body parts.

Rule 4: Walk for at least one hour per day

This might sound like it's a lot, but it's really not. You can walk for 10 minutes, 6 times per day and this could be divided into even smaller chunks. By making sure you are actually out there doing something, you can interrupt that anxiety cycle before it begins.

Rule 5: No coffee for 8 hours before bed

Coffee is actually a drug, and we need to start treating it as such.

The bad thing is that coffee can worsen your anxiety and we have a lot of tolerance for it. It starts with a few cups, and it becomes a whole jug. By ensuring you do not get any caffeine before you sleep, you ensure that your sleep quality is not compromised.

Rule 6: Posture up

One of the things that anxiety makes us do is get in the dreaded fetal position. We all feel like doing it sometimes. Crouch down, protect our neck and stomach, and curl up into a ball. While this might make you feel safe, it's actually doing a lot more harm than you think. Instead, you should lift your chest up, chin nice and straight, shoulders back, and eyes looking in front of you. This is the body language of a confident person and although you do not feel confident while doing it at first, it's kind of a 'fake it 'til you make it' situation where the act itself makes you feel confident.

Rule 7: No more than one hour of social media per day

The general rule here is to stay informed, but not too informed. We used to think that the more we know, the better we do. In reality, the more we know, the less we actually know. Having a constant stream of information coming your way all the time is not a good idea, and chances are that you are not going to use any of that information for a good purpose. Here is the kicker; news outlets, social media, and internet posts are literally designed to grab your attention and give you some of that anxiety so you will stop what you are doing and read more. This isn't good for your mental health, which is why you should probably do no more than one hour of social media per day.

Rule 8: Track your life

One of the elements that we lose as we age is time. The older we grow, the less we tend to think of our past and this can come at a price. Having a journal where you can write practical things you did in life is so useful in the future. In addition to that, we all love that feeling when we get in a time machine reading those old cringeworthy notes we wrote when we were younger. Moreover, having a journal can also help you track how you feel and how you are progressing with each method you are using so that you know which one is working.

Rule 9: Work on your body

You may not realize this, but your body might be giving you a lot of anxiety. Stress can cause muscles to get tight, which creates pulling forces on your neck, shoulders, chest, and hips. All of these areas can get very tense and cause your anxiety to spike. Therefore, make sure you exercise regularly and that you have a few massages every once in a while.

Rule 10: Be the spectator in your mind

Whenever you feel the anxiety starting to intensify, instead of just falling victim to it, watch it all unfold. Look at how your anxiety started, how it made you feel, and what were the breaking when you started to fall prey to the anxiety. By being the spectator in your head, you can see things differently and even give yourself a clue as to how you can tame anxious thoughts.

The bottom line:

Anxiety sure is tough, but it's not unbeatable. There are a lot of tools in your arsenal that can be used to treat and battle anxiety. You can combine chemical intervention with lifestyle changes which will have a huge impact on the way you think. Not mention, it's a great stepping-stone for your self-improvement journey.

CHAPTER 6

The change is now

Whether you are reading this at your desk and taking notes or reading this in your bed, it's important to know that anxiety needs to be fixed as soon as possible. Regardless of what you are doing at this moment, there is a big chance you can do something to improve your situation. If you are reading this at 1 am and you have to wake up early, then drop this and finish later so you can get better sleep. If you are at your desk, start taking notes and analyzing your situation. If you're about to cook, throw some vegetables into the mix with some fruit, go for a walk, and stay active. The point of this final chapter is to get you going, because that is the most important thing. We want to move from a passive inactive anxiety state into a state where you are doing something that can inch you closer to your goal.

The anti-anxiety strategy:

It's important to go into this with a clear and decisive plan. The reason for that is because a plan lets you know the main components of the strategy. In addition to that, it gives you a clear target that you can tackle instead of just aiming at nowhere. So, let's get started.

The anti-anxiety worksheet:

Review a common scenario that causes your anxiety to trigger

Can be talking in front of a crowd

The main goal of this is to get your brain to know the anxious thoughts and how they play out.

Think of yourself in the anxiety-triggering scenario that was just outlined.

What is the worst-case scenario that can happen in this situation?

The purpose of this box is to outline your fears and what you think might happen. It's important to actually see and make your fears come true on paper. This gets you to a point where you can spectate over your fears instead of falling prey to them.

Now, talk about what is the most likely true scenario that you can guess will happen

Now, talk about what is the most likely true scenario that you can guess will happen

By talking about what you think will likely happen, the worst-case scenario goes from being "potentially real" to unlikely.

<u>What do you believe is the best-case scenario in this situation</u>

It's important to not only weigh out the negative thoughts but also the positive ones as well. By including a section where you talk about what the best-case scenario could be, your reality shifts a little bit. Instead of thinking about what you fear could happen, you will start to talk about what you want to happen.

<u>Coming face to face with your fears:</u>

<u>If the worst-case scenario were to happen right now, how would it concern you today?</u>

You cannot hide from your fears because anxiety feeds on fear. Instead, you should not be afraid to look at your fears and come face to face with the worst-case scenario.

<u>List three bad things that could happen if the bad scenario were to happen. Now list three good things that could happen with the good scenario:</u>

Rewiring the anxious brain:

Rewiring the brain has a lot to do with how we can change our thought patterns. This can be done by changing our thoughts mentally, or through altering our brain structure somehow.

Neuroplasticity and anxiety in the brain:

The brain is an extremely complex organ that we still don't know a lot about. It can do some of the most interesting things and it still surprises us. There have been cases when people made their brain use different parts to operate their limbs after trauma to the brain (Taub et al. 2006). This means that the brain does not always use the same connections for the same purposes and that the brain can be a lot more flexible. For example, exercise is one of the areas that show a lot of promise in the way we use brain cells. Generally speaking, a bigger muscle is a stronger muscle, but strength is not always about size. It might seem like strength is a deviation from rewiring the brain, but strength is merely recruiting muscle mass to produce force. Anxiety recruits the brain to get into the fight or flight response. Research has shown that exercise can actually strengthen connections in the brain. By making the brain more capable of connecting with the whole body, muscles are able to contract a lot harder and more in unison (Cotman and Berchtold 2002).

The brain has shown that it can be a lot more flexible and adaptive to its circumstances than previously thought. By training the brain to work in unison with things such as in exercise or playing a musical instrument, we can create new connections. This shows that the brain can be rewired and reshaped regardless of what age you are. The organic structure of the brain may be predetermined by your genes, but this does not mean you cannot change it.

Cortex anxiety and amygdala anxiety:

Let us talk about the two pathways of anxiety in the brain and what we can do it about them. The cortex-based anxiety is the one that relates to sensation, logic, reason, thoughts, memory, and planning. Most anxiety treatments go after this pathway. The reason for that is because cortex anxiety is more conscious.

On the other hand, amygdala-based anxiety is more of a pathway that relates to the physical effects that anxiety has on your body. The thing is, amygdala-based anxiety is a lot trickier to treat as it's less conscious and more instinctual. For instance, the amygdala will mobilize bodily reactions in a fraction of a second before you even realize it and it will spike your adrenaline, contract your muscles, and increase your heart rate and blood pressure all at once. In other words, the amygdala does not care about what you think, it just does things as it pleases. For example, if you see a raging pit bull with blood running down its mouth coming at you full force, you're not going to deduce the fact that there is a 90 percent chance of you getting mauled if you do not run. The amygdala kicks in and gets you running faster than you thought you could ever run, your instincts sharpen, and you think of a million thoughts just to evade the danger.

While some doctors focus on the cortex, meaning how you can logically make sense of anxiety, other health practitioners focus on sedating the amygdala using medications such as alprazolam and clonazepam.

The amygdala is always on the lookout for potential dangers and always there for you when you need it. On the other hand, cortex-based anxiety focuses on the thought build-up. For instance, getting anxious over forgetting that you might have left the stove turned on.

This is a logical thought because you are thinking about the potential danger of your house catching fire. But amygdala-based anxiety is like when you see an angry face shouting at you. The amygdala does not need you to analyze the face because it knows that this is a face of danger and speeds your heart rate up to protect you. In addition to that, the amygdala can use emotional memory when identifying danger. For instance, someone might have anxiety when they are in the passenger seat of the car because they had an accident when they were next to the driver.

Here comes the tricky part. The way to hijack the amygdala and rewire it is not through hours of therapy or reading books; it's through experience. While you might have success with cortex-based anxiety by reading books or going to therapy, you will likely have no success using the same strategy with the amygdala. This is because the amygdala is about experiences. No amount of book reading is going to get you over the fear of pit bulls; instead, you have to actually be with pit bulls for a long time and create a bond with them to the point that your amygdala does not recognize them as a threat.

The bottom line:

It's important to work on anxiety right now and not waste any more time. Anxiety is good at making you stagnate and stay in your place. Therefore, you have to make an effort to move forward. The more you do, the less you have to struggle with anxiety. Find ways to rewire your anxiety, addressing both ways that anxiety is triggered. Use the anti-anxiety worksheet so you can assess your anxiety level at different times and for different situations. Anxiety can be conquered if you do something about it, whether that thing you do gets you closer by an inch or a mile, progress is still progress.

References:

Dunbar, R. I. M. (1992). *Neocortex size as a constraint on group size in primates. Journal of Human Evolution, 22(6), 469–493.* doi:10.1016/0047-2484(92)90081-j

Hirschtritt, M. E., Lee, P. C., Pauls, D. L., Dion, Y., Grados, M. A., Illmann, C., King, R. A., Sandor, P., McMahon, W. M., Lyon, G. J., Cath, D. C., Kurlan, R., Robertson, M. M., Osiecki, L., Scharf, J. M., Mathews, C. A., & Tourette Syndrome Association International Consortium for Genetics (2015). Lifetime prevalence, age of risk, and genetic relationships of comorbid psychiatric disorders in Tourette syndrome. JAMA Psychiatry, 72(4), 325–333. https://doi.org/10.1001/jamapsychiatry.2014.2650

Raison, C. L., & Miller, A. H. (2012). The evolutionary significance of depression in Pathogen Host Defense (PATHOS-D). Molecular Psychiatry, 18(1), 15–37. doi:10.1038/mp.2012.2

Milham, M. P., Nugent, A. C., Drevets, W. C., Dickstein, D. P., Leibenluft, E., Ernst, M., Charney, D., & Pine, D. S. (2005). Selective reduction in amygdala volume in pediatric anxiety disorders: a voxel-based morphometry investigation. Biological psychiatry, 57(9), 961–966. https://doi.org/10.1016/j.biopsych.2005.01.038

Neumeister, A. (2004). Reduced Serotonin Type 1A Receptor Binding in Panic Disorder. Journal of Neuroscience, 24(3), 589–591. doi:10.1523/jneurosci.4921-03.2004

Bremner JD, Elzinga B, Schmahl C, Vermetten E. Structural and functional plasticity of the human brain in posttraumatic stress disorder. Prog Brain Res. 2008;167:171-186. doi:10.1016/S0079-

6123(07)67012-5

Martin, E. I., Ressler, K. J., Binder, E., & Nemeroff, C. B. (2009). The Neurobiology of Anxiety Disorders: Brain Imaging, Genetics, and Psychoneuroendocrinology. Psychiatric Clinics of North America, 32(3), 549–575. doi:10.1016/j.psc.2009.05.004

Cotman, C. W., and N. C. Berchtold. 2002. "Exercise: A Behavioral

Intervention to Enhance Brain Health and Plasticity." Trends in

Neurosciences 25:295–301.

Taub, E., G. Uswatte, D. K. King, D. Morris, J. E. Crago, and A.

Chatterjee. 2006. "A Placebo-Controlled Trial of Constraint Induced Movement Therapy for Upper Extremity After Stroke."

Stroke 37:1045–1049.

Printed in Great Britain
by Amazon

22475355R00030